HISTORIC BUILDINGS OF NEW YORK CITY

A Coloring Book of Architecture

by Scott Clowney

APPLEWOOD BOOKS
an imprint of Arcadia Publishing

INTRODUCTON

The anticipation and excitement I felt as a teenager leading up to my first visit to New York City was palpable. The Big Apple's skyscrapers, people, and energy were everything I wanted to experience as a young farm boy captivated by the city and what it meant to live and work there. I knew architecture was the subject of my dreams when the New York City skyline came into view for the first time.

Life in the city is filled with variety, from classic yellow taxis to city subway cars and budget-friendly street vendors to expensive five-star restaurants. From Central Park walks to Rockefeller Center views and Broadway musicals to people watching in Times Square—the allure of New York City is like no other. Some of my favorite experiences include museum hopping and street photography, discovering famous artworks at the Met and MoMA, and grabbing a camera and capturing black-and-white scenes of urban life on the city's active streets.

I've visited New York many times over 25 years, but I rarely traveled beyond Manhattan. Since I couldn't possibly represent the plethora of historic landmarks and hidden hot spots throughout the city's five boroughs, this book highlights points of interest in Manhattan: usual suspects like the Chrysler Building, Grand Central Terminal, and the Solomon R. Guggenheim Museum; lesser-known subjects like Central Synagogue, the former Lord & Taylor Building at 901 Broadway, and the Merchant's House Museum.

One of the most densely populated cities in the world, New York City is a cultural hub with magnetic appeal. Its iconic landmarks, lively spaces, and diverse inhabitants challenge us to think critically about urban life. I hope this book encourages you to connect with the city in a way that is informative and engaging. I hope it also inspires you to appreciate the significance of historic buildings and the creative minds who helped shape them into enduring structures.

—Scott Clowney

Dedication
To the spirit of extraordinary people whose vision, craft, and determination continue to shape this beloved city.

Acknowledgments
Thanks to my family and friends in New York City for their hospitality and support.
Special thanks to the team at Applewood Books.

ISBN 978-1-64194-002-3

Published by Applewood Books, Inc.
an imprint of Arcadia Publishing

Visit Scott Clowney on the web at www.scottclowney.com

Printed in the United States of America

CONTENTS

ELLIS ISLAND NATIONAL MUSEUM OF IMMIGRATION

LOCATION: Statue of Liberty National Monument

NEIGHBORHOOD: Upper New York Bay

ARCHITECTS: Edward Tilton and William Boring

Identified by several titles in its lifetime, Ellis Island is located south of Manhattan off the New Jersey coastline in the Upper New York Bay. In the 1600s, it was known as Gibbet Island, where men convicted of piracy were hanged. Named for Samuel Ellis, who purchased the island around the Revolutionary War, the island was later selected as a processing center for immigrants beginning in the early 1890s.

ALEXANDER HAMILTON U.S. CUSTOM HOUSE

LOCATION: 1 Bowling Green

NEIGHBORHOOD: Financial District

ARCHITECT: Cass Gilbert

This building is named for Alexander Hamilton, the first U.S. secretary of the treasury (1789–95), whose portrait appears on the ten-dollar bill. Located on the former site of Fort Amsterdam, at the southern tip of Manhattan, this ornate Beaux-Arts building was completed in 1907 to house the Port of New York's duty and tax collection operations. On the exterior, four allegorical female statues represent international commerce between America, Europe, Asia, and Africa. They were carved by the American sculptor Daniel Chester French. In the 1990s, the building was restored and renovated to house the National Museum of the American Indian, George Gustav Heye Center.

U·S·CUSTOM·HOUSE
TRANSFORMER

FRAUNCES TAVERN

LOCATION: 54 Pearl Street

NEIGHBORHOOD: Financial District

ARCHITECTS: Unknown (1719– construction and various renovations); William Mersereau (1906–07 restoration)

The original structure was built in 1719 to serve as the residence of Etienne "Stephen" Delancey, a wealthy merchant in colonial New York. In 1762, the American patriot Samuel Fraunces bought the building from Delancey's descendants and turned it into a tavern. Here, in 1783, General George Washington famously bade farewell to his officers before his short-lived retirement in Mount Vernon, Virginia. The building served thereafter as government offices, a bake house, dry-goods store, grocery store, and boardinghouse. Over time, it also underwent many architectural changes, due in part to several fires. The Sons of the Revolution purchased the building in 1904, reconstructed it a few years later amid controversy, and opened it as the Fraunces Tavern Museum.

Broad St
DO NOT
ENTER

NEW YORK STOCK EXCHANGE (NYSE)

LOCATION: 18 Broad Street

NEIGHBORHOOD: Financial District

ARCHITECTS: George B. Post (1901–03); Trowbridge & Livingston

Architect George Post won a competition to design the new 1903 New York Stock Exchange building. A monument to American capitalism, the Broad Street façade resembles a Roman temple, with a symmetrical portico comprised of fluted Corinthian columns, entablature, and a pediment with statuary designed by John Quincy Adams Ward and Paul Wayland Bartlett. The NYSE is famous for its use of bells to signal the opening and closing of trading each day. Originally performed by floor managers, the bells have been rung by guests such as executives, world leaders, and celebrities since the mid-1950s.

NEW YORK STOCK EXCHANGE
NYSE
MCMI

FEDERAL HALL NATIONAL MEMORIAL

LOCATION: 26 Wall Street

NEIGHBORHOOD: Financial District

ARCHITECTS: Alexander Jackson Davis and Ithiel Town with John Frazee and Samuel Thompson (1842); Einhorn Yaffee Prescott Architecture & Engineering (2006 restoration)

City Hall, the original building on this site, was remodeled by Pierre Charles L'Enfant to house the first executive, legislative, and judicial branches of the government when New York became the first capital of the United States. The building was renamed Federal Hall in 1788 and, on April 30, 1789, George Washington was inaugurated here as the country's first president. When Congress moved to Philadelphia soon after, the building returned to the government of New York City until it was razed in 1812. The current Greek Revival building was completed in 1842 to serve as a Customs House for the Port of New York. The statue of George Washington by John Quincy Adams Ward was erected in 1882. The building was designated as a National Historic Site in 1939.

TRINITY CHURCH

LOCATION: 75 Broadway

NEIGHBORHOOD: Financial District

ARCHITECTS: Richard Upjohn (1839–46); Murphy Burnham & Buttrick Architects (2018– restoration)

A registered National Historic Landmark, the current Trinity Church (one of three on the site) was designed by British-born American architect Richard Upjohn, who cofounded the American Institute of Architects in the late 1850s. Completed in 1846, the 281-foot-high steeple made it the tallest building in the United States until surpassed by St. Michael's Church in Chicago in 1869. Upjohn designed the church in a Gothic Revival style. Among other notable figures, Alexander Hamilton, first secretary of the treasury under President George Washington, is buried in Trinity Church Cemetery.

Broadway

ST. PAUL'S CHAPEL

LOCATION: 209 Broadway

NEIGHBORHOOD: Financial District

ARCHITECTS: Thomas McBean with master craftsman Andrew Gautier (1766); James Crommelin Lawrence (1794 tower); Murphy Burnham & Buttrick Architects (2016– restoration)

Considered the oldest surviving ecclesiastical building in Manhattan, this historic landmark was built in 1766 as a supporting chapel for nearby Trinity Church. In 1776, Trinity Church was destroyed by the Great Fire of New York. St. Paul's survived and served as a house of prayer for many notable figures in the community, including George Washington, who attended services after taking the oath of office at Federal Hall. The pulpit and Pierre Charles L'Enfant–designed altarpiece are considered additions from the late 1780s.

IHS

ONE WORLD TRADE CENTER

LOCATION: 285 Fulton Street

NEIGHBORHOOD: Financial District

ARCHITECTS: David M. Childs and T. J. Gottesdiener of Skidmore, Owings & Merrill LLP

MASTER PLAN: Studio Daniel Libeskind

Out of tragedy, One World Trade Center was conceived in a plan to rebuild the World Trade Center site following the terrorist attacks of September 11, 2001. Completed in 2014, after a lengthy design and construction process, the tower rises from a concrete core designed for safety and security. The footprint is identical to the base of the original Twin Towers. The height, including a 408-foot-high spire, reaches a symbolic 1,776 feet to reference the year the Declaration of Independence was signed. One World Trade Center is part of a larger complex of buildings, including the National September 11 Memorial & Museum.

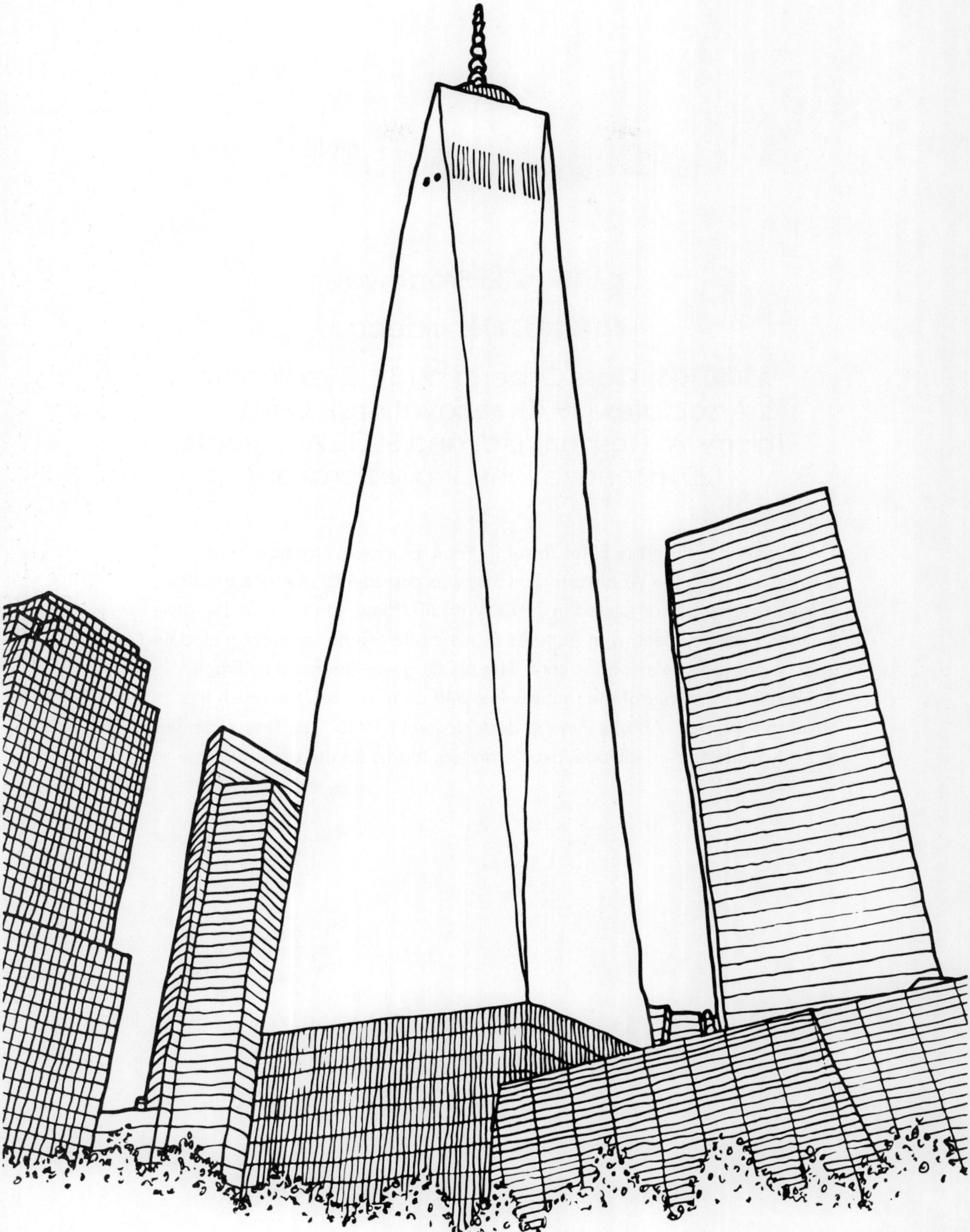

WOOLWORTH BUILDING

LOCATION: 233 Broadway

NEIGHBORHOOD: Tribeca

ARCHITECTS: Cass Gilbert (1913); Ehrenkrantz & Associates (1970s renovations); Office of Thierry W. Despont Ltd. and SLCE Architects (2018 renovations and restoration)

Though shorter than the Eiffel Tower in Paris, France, a structure that opened in 1889, the Woolworth Building was considered the tallest building in the world when completed in 1913. With 60 floors, the Neo-Gothic–style building rises 792 feet, with features that include ornate terra-cotta cladding, tracery, and gargoyles on the roof. The building was financed by Frank W. Woolworth, owner of the famous five-and-dime retailer, for which the building is named. An observation deck closed in 1945. The skyscraper was recently renovated to include luxury condominiums on the upper floors.

WOOLWORTH
BUILDING
233

BROOKLYN BRIDGE

LOCATION: East River

ENGINEERS: John Augustus Roebling (1867–69); Washington Augustus Roebling and Emily Warren Roebling (1869–83)

A hybrid cable-stayed and suspension bridge, the nearly 6,000-foot-long Brooklyn Bridge spans the East River to connect Brooklyn with Manhattan. It is considered the first structure to use steel cables in construction, a technique credited to the German-born American engineer John A. Roebling. When Roebling died from injuries sustained on-site, his son and daughter-in-law completed the bridge after 14 years of construction. On May 24, 1883, the bridge opened, but history records that American showman P. T. Barnum led elephants and camels across the bridge the following year to squelch concerns of structural defects. Today, the bridge carries about 150,000 vehicles and pedestrians every day.

MERCHANT'S HOUSE MUSEUM

LOCATION: 29 East 4th Street

NEIGHBORHOOD: NoHo

ARCHITECTS: Joseph Brewster (1831–32); Joseph Roberto with Carolyn Roberto (1971 restoration)

Built 1832 in what was once a suburb of the city, this building is considered the most-preserved 19th-century family house in New York City, with original furniture and family memorabilia. The exterior is considered Federal in appearance, but the interiors are regarded as fine examples of Greek Revival architecture. The house was purchased by Seabury Tredwell, a merchant, in 1835, whose descendants lived there for nearly 100 years. The house became a museum in 1935 and was designated a New York City Landmark 30 years later after the Landmarks Preservation Commission was formed. It is also a National Historic Landmark.

901 BROADWAY (LORD & TAYLOR BUILDING)

LOCATION: 901 Broadway

NEIGHBORHOOD: Flatiron District

ARCHITECTS: James H. Giles (1869–70); RAND Engineering & Architecture, DPC (2011 exterior restoration)

This five-story cast-iron New York City Landmark opened 1870 in the Flatiron District. The neighborhood was populated with department stores selling fashionable clothes and luxury goods at the time in what was known as the "Ladies Mile." Originally home to the upscale dry-goods store Lord & Taylor, it was part of a larger structure whose southern massing was later demolished when the store moved to its Fifth Avenue location. Used thereafter for manufacturing and left vacant for many years, the building fell into disrepair until new ownerships funded renovations beginning in the 1990s.

E 20 St

FLATIRON BUILDING

LOCATION: 175 5th Avenue

NEIGHBORHOOD: Flatiron District

ARCHITECTS: Daniel Burnham and Frederick P. Dinkelberg of D. H. Burnham & Co. (1901–02); Hurley & Farinella (1991 façade restoration)

Completed in 1902, this unusual three-sided structure was originally named the Fuller Building after the George A. Fuller Company, which erected the building and headquartered there. Fuller, who was based in Chicago, is credited as the "father of the modern skyscraper" and the inventor of the concept of general contracting. Designed by renowned Chicago architect Daniel Burnham, the Beaux-Arts–style Flatiron Building is a steel-frame building clad in limestone and glazed terra-cotta. The triangular footprint, only six feet wide at its smallest end, was said to worry critics, who dubbed the building "Burnham's Folly" for fear it would collapse.

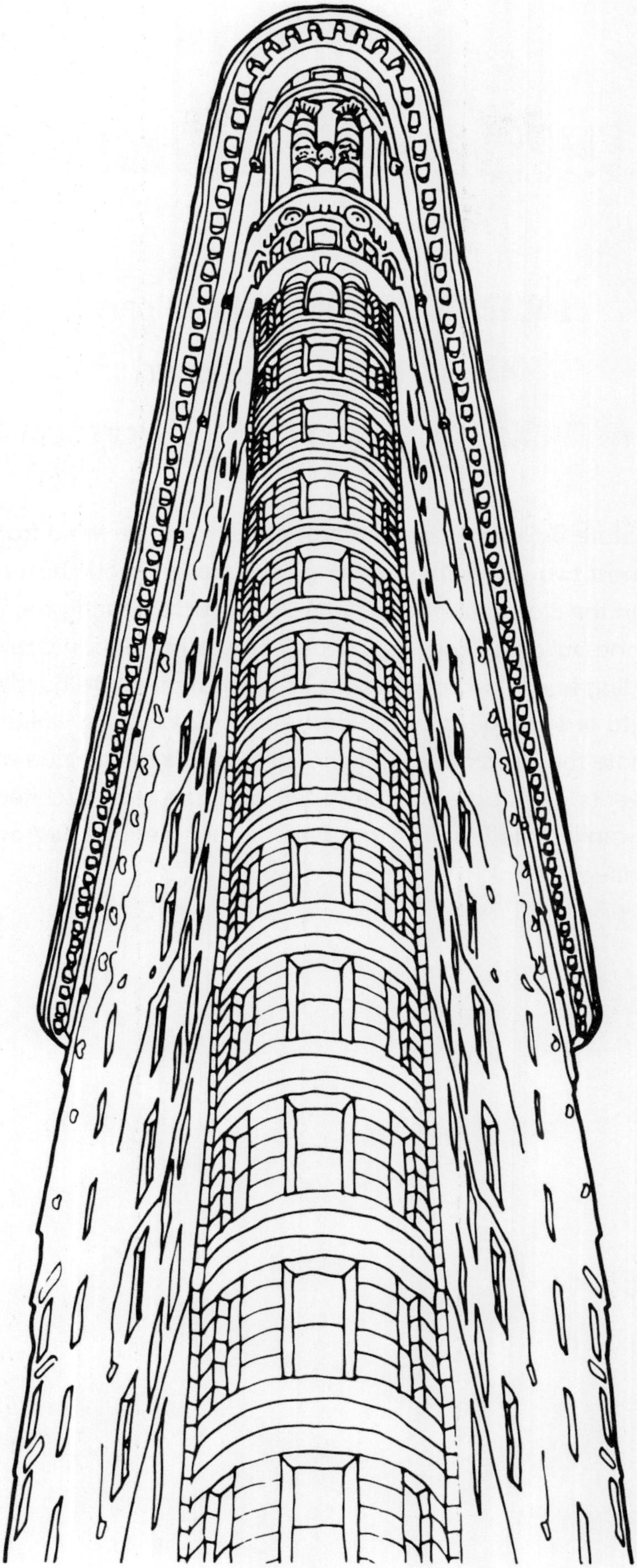

EMPIRE STATE BUILDING

LOCATION: 20 West 34th Street

NEIGHBORHOOD: Midtown

ARCHITECTS: Shreve, Lamb & Harmon

The Empire State Building was the tallest building in the world from 1931 to 1970. Almost two years after opening, it made cinematic history when it appeared in the classic film *King Kong*. Constructed during the Great Depression, the building's owners failed to secure more than a few tenants and the building briefly became known as the "Empty State Building." Today, visitors flock to observatories on the 86th and 102nd floors, while the tower lights illuminate the city skyline with changing colors to coincide with holidays and world events. Conducted by the American Institute of Architects in 2007, a public poll ranked the Empire State Building number one as America's Favorite Architecture.

THE MORGAN LIBRARY & MUSEUM

LOCATION: 225 Madison Avenue at East 36th Street

NEIGHBORHOOD: Murray Hill

ARCHITECTS: Charles Follen McKim of McKim, Mead & White (1902–06); Renzo Piano Building Workshop (2006 expansion); Unknown (2010 interior restoration); Beyer Blinder Belle with Integrated Conservation Resources, Inc. (2016 exterior restoration)

Renowned architect Charles McKim planned this small building, inspired by Italian Renaissance design and completed in 1906, to serve as financier Pierpont Morgan's private library. Regarded for its integration of architecture, painting, and sculpture, the library became a public institution in 1924 under the direction of J. P. Morgan Jr. Morgan's extensive collection of books, manuscripts, prints, and rare holdings were then accessible as resources to a wide audience. The interior is richly ornamented, including the rotunda, whose decoration is attributed to Harry Siddons Mowbray. Today, The Morgan Library & Museum has evolved into a landmark destination celebrated for art appreciation and scholarly research.

NEW YORK PUBLIC LIBRARY, STEPHEN A. SCHWARZMAN BUILDING

LOCATION: 476 5th Avenue

NEIGHBORHOOD: Midtown

ARCHITECT: Carrère and Hastings

Referred to as the main branch, this Beaux-Arts–style building took more than a decade to complete, at a cost of $9 million. The renowned New York City–based architects designed everything, including the lights, interior furniture, and hardware. President William Howard Taft presided over the official dedication on May 23, 1911. The third-floor, 23,000-square-foot Rose Main Reading Room, a public space with landmark status, welcomes historians, scholars, readers, and writers in an architecturally rich setting under ornate 52-foot-high ceilings.

GRAND CENTRAL TERMINAL

LOCATION: 89 East 42nd Street

NEIGHBORHOOD: Midtown

ARCHITECTS: Reed & Stem and Warren & Wetmore (1913); Beyer Blinder Belle (1990–present renovations)

Grand Central Terminal opened in 1913, less than three years after the McKim, Mead & White–designed Pennsylvania Station opened. Expressed by grand interior spaces, monumental exterior proportions, and fine detailing throughout, this Beaux-Arts–style structure is an iconic New York City landmark. Almost demolished, a fate realized by Pennsylvania Station in 1963, the terminal was saved through a preservation campaign that ultimately involved the Supreme Court. Jacqueline Kennedy Onassis was a leading spokesperson.

MetLife
GRAND CENTRAL TERMINAL
GRAND CENTRAL TERMINAL

CHRYSLER BUILDING

LOCATION: 405 Lexington Avenue

NEIGHBORHOOD: Midtown East

ARCHITECT: William Van Alen (1928–30)

ENGINEERS: Thornton Tomasetti (2001–03 restoration)

Financed by Walter P. Chrysler, founder of Chrysler Corporation, the Chrysler Building was the first skyscraper to reach more than 1,000 feet when it was completed in 1930. Designed in the Art Deco style, it is characterized by stepped massing with metallic embellishments, including eagle-shaped gargoyles and radiator-cap hood ornaments found on Chrysler automobiles. The terraced crown, its most iconic feature, is clad in stainless steel and topped with a 125-foot-high spire. In the early 1930s, photojournalist Margaret Bourke-White maintained a studio inside the Chrysler Building and famously had herself photographed on one of the gargoyles projecting out from the building on the 61st floor.

UNITED NATIONS HEADQUARTERS

LOCATION: 760 United Nations Plaza

NEIGHBORHOOD: Turtle Bay

ARCHITECTS: Wallace K. Harrison with various international architects (1948–52)

Led by architect Wallace Harrison of Harrison & Abramovitz, an international team of architects planned this iconic International Style complex on 18 acres of land overlooking the East River. Among the group were Swiss-French architect Le Corbusier and Brazilian architect Oscar Niemeyer, whose two design schemes were selected to create one final design. The core of the project is expressed by Niemeyer's rectangular, tower-like Secretariat Building rising 39 floors over the site and Le Corbusier's low-rise, 1,800-seat General Assembly Hall (hidden from view in the drawing).

CENTRAL SYNAGOGUE

LOCATION: 652 Lexington Avenue

NEIGHBORHOOD: Midtown East

ARCHITECTS: Henry Fernbach (1870–72); Ely Jacques Kahn (1946–49 renovations); Hardy Holzman Pfeiffer Associates (1998–2001 restoration)

Dedicated in 1872, Central Synagogue is considered the oldest synagogue in continuous use in New York City. It was designed by Henry Fernbach, New York's first prominent Jewish architect, whose design was inspired by the Dohány Street Synagogue in Budapest, Hungary. In a Moorish Revival style, the building contains polychrome decorations of geometric patterns and stenciling throughout. The main entrance sits below a large rose window, and two octagonal minaret towers support shimmering copper-clad spheres. In 1998, a fire destroyed the interior and, after extensive renovations, the synagogue was rededicated in 2001 just two days prior to the September 11 attacks.

ST. PATRICK'S CATHEDRAL

LOCATION: 5th Avenue and 51st Street

NEIGHBORHOOD: Midtown

ARCHITECTS: James Renwick Jr. (1879); Maginnis & Walsh (1942 renovations); Murphy Burnham & Buttrick Architects (2006–2017 conservation and restoration)

In 1858, the cornerstone was laid for St. Patrick's Cathedral, seat of the archdiocese of New York. The cathedral opened in 1879, but it was fully completed in 1888 with the addition of 330-foot-high twin spires. Designed with Tuckahoe marble, a stone found in upper Manhattan, the Bronx, and Westchester County known for its quality and purity of color, the Neo-Gothic style cathedral is sited on a full city block and accommodates up to 3,000 people. Repaired and restored many times throughout its history, it recently underwent a multiphase restoration process that included stone repairs and cleaning on the exterior and interior surfaces, as well as the addition of a new geothermal system to heat and cool the building.

COMCAST BUILDING (30 ROCKEFELLER PLAZA)

LOCATION: 45 Rockefeller Plaza

NEIGHBORHOOD: Midtown

ARCHITECTS: Raymond Hood with Wallace K. Harrison, Harvey Wiley Corbett, and Reinhard and Hofmeister (1932–33); Unknown (2014 interior renovations)

BUILDER: John R. Todd

Previously known as the RCA Building and General Electric Building, this skyscraper was developed by philanthropist John D. Rockefeller Jr. in the 1930s during the Great Depression. With verticality and stepped massing, the design is characteristic of the Art Deco style popular at the time for its streamlined aesthetic. Flanked by allegorical figures Light and Sound, sculptor Lee Lawrie's panel above the center entry is known as Wisdom. Today, Rockefeller Center is comprised of 19 buildings (last building completed in 1940) on 22 acres and serves as the East Coast headquarters of NBCUniversal, a subsidiary of Comcast Corporation, which owns and operates shows like *Nightly News* and *Saturday Night Live*.

WISDOM AND KNOWLEDGE
SHALL BE THE
STABILITY OF THY TIMES

RADIO CITY MUSIC HALL

LOCATION: 1260 6th Avenue

NEIGHBORHOOD: Midtown

ARCHITECT: Edward Durell Stone

INTERIOR DESIGNER: Donald Deskey

Radio City Music Hall opened in 1932 during the Great Depression, built on the site of what was intended to be an opera house for the Metropolitan Opera Company. Despite hard times, the music hall thrived for decades with concerts, live stage performances, and film screenings. It was financed by the American financier and philanthropist John D. Rockefeller Jr. and is part of the larger Rockefeller Center complex. Named for its original tenant, the Radio Corporation of America, the music hall is a fine example of the Art Deco style and home of the Rockettes, an American precision dance company.

RADIO CITY
MUSIC HALL
RADIO CITY
Music Hall
MUSIC HALL
CHASE

CARNEGIE HALL

LOCATION: 57th Street and Seventh Avenue

NEIGHBORHOOD: Midtown

ARCHITECTS: William B. Tuthill with consulting architects Richard Morris Hunt and Dankmar Adler (1890–91); Polshek Partnership Architects (1986–2003 renovations); César Pelli & Associates (1987–89 Carnegie Hall Tower addition); Iu+ Bibliowicz Architects (2010–14 Studio Towers renovation)

Financed by the Scottish-born American industrialist and philanthropist Andrew Carnegie, Carnegie Hall (originally called Music Hall) opened in 1891 as a concert venue, with seating for nearly 3,700 patrons in three auditoriums. The Main Hall is famous for its near perfect acoustical properties. Tchaikovsky conducted on opening night. On October 25, 1944, at the age of 76, Florence Foster Jenkins, known as the "singer who couldn't sing," made her debut at Carnegie Hall. When the Lincoln Center for the Performing Arts was constructed just blocks away, Carnegie Hall was in danger of demolition, but the city purchased the building and it was later designated a National Historic Landmark in 1962.

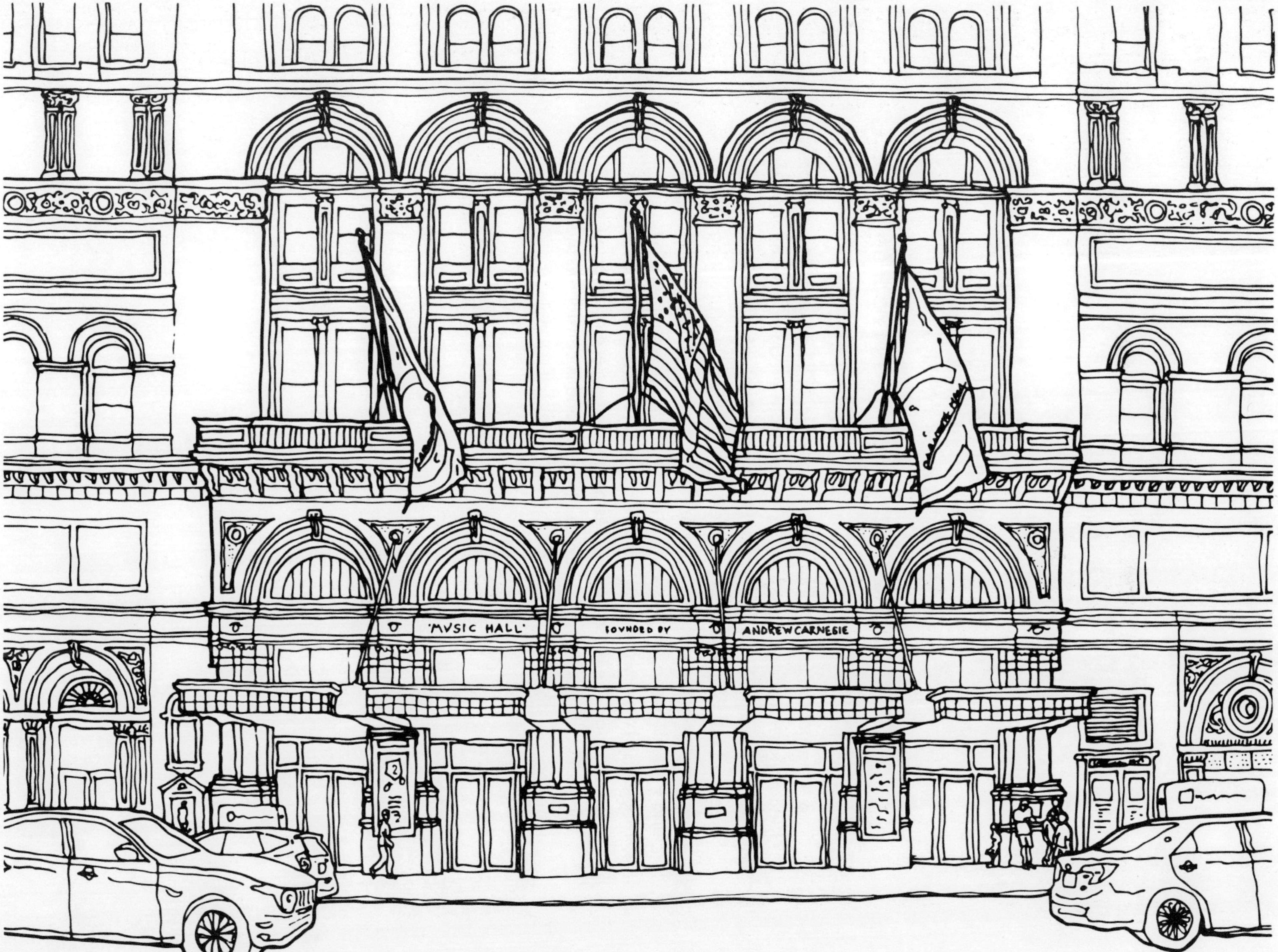
'MUSIC HALL'
FOUNDED BY
ANDREW CARNEGIE

METROPOLITAN OPERA HOUSE

LOCATION: 30 Lincoln Center Plaza

NEIGHBORHOOD: Upper West Side

ARCHITECT: Wallace K. Harrison (1963–66)

The Metropolitan Opera House was founded in 1883 as an artistic platform for composers, conductors, and performers from around the world. When it joined the Lincoln Center for the Performing Arts with other institutions, it opened in 1966 as the Lincoln Center, a vast complex consisting of many buildings designed by many architects, among them Eero Saarinen and Philip Johnson. Unlike traditional European opera houses, the Modernist 14-story Met, with its iconic façade of five arched openings and Mondrian-like glass wall, serves as the centerpiece of Lincoln Center. The Met holds nearly 4,000 people at a time and is considered the largest repertory auditorium in the world.

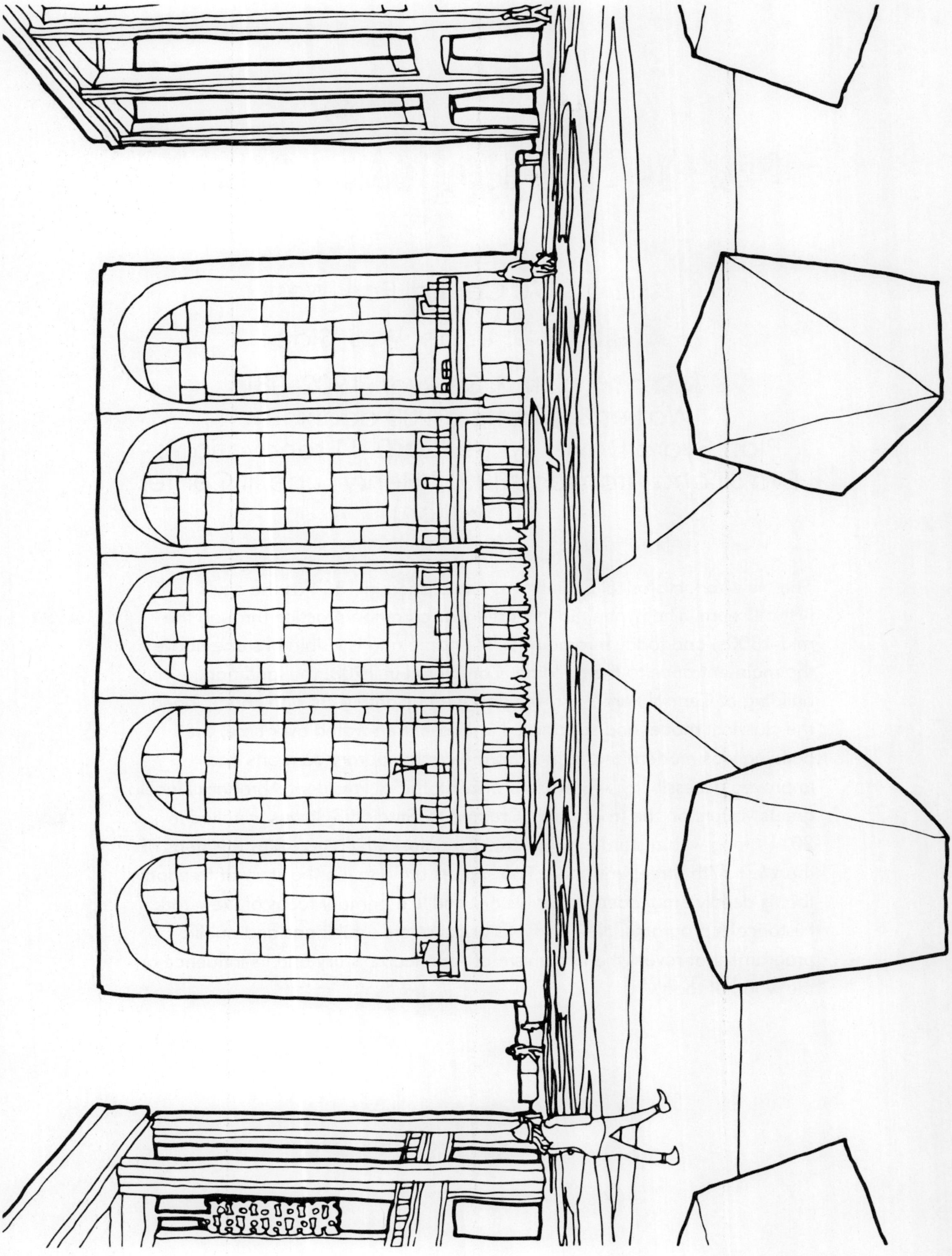

NEW-YORK HISTORICAL SOCIETY

LOCATION: 170 Central Park West

NEIGHBORHOOD: Upper West Side

ARCHITECTS: York & Sawyer (1902–08); Walker & Gillette (1938 addition); Platt Byard Dovell White (2010–11 renovation); Eva Jiřičná Architects (2017 Henry Luce III Center renovation)

The New-York Historical Society was established in 1804 as the city's first museum. The hyphen in its name was common practice through the mid-1800s, and today it remains in the name and is visible in stone above the main entrance to the building. Completed in 1908, the landmark building at Central Park West was designed by architects who championed the classical model and specialized in banks. Renovated over time, the building was modernized to incorporate contemporary comforts and improved accessibility. A life-size bronze statue of President Abraham Lincoln greets visitors on the front steps. Created by StudioEIS, it was installed in 2011 along with a statue of Frederick Douglass which occupies the steps of the West 77th Street entrance. The statues bring to life the story of freedom that is deeply embedded in our history and is a primary focus of New-York Historical's programs. New-York Historical offers exhibitions and public programs that reveal the dynamism of American history and its influence on the world of today.

AMERICAN MUSEUM OF NATURAL HISTORY

LOCATION: Central Park West at 79th Street

NEIGHBORHOOD: Upper West Side

ARCHITECTS: Calvert Vaux and J. Wrey Mould (1874–77); J. Cleaveland Cady (77th Street façade); John Russell Pope (1929-1936 Central Park West façade); Kevin Roche John Dinkeloo and Associates (fourth-floor Fossil Halls); Polshek Partnership Architects, now Ennead Architects LLP (Rose Center for Earth and Space); Wiss, Janney, Elstner Associates, Inc. (2009 restoration of 77th Street façade); Studio Gang (2019– Richard Gilder Center for Science, Education, and Innovation, facing Columbus Avenue)

Part of the New York State Memorial to Theodore Roosevelt, the Central Park West façade of the American Museum of Natural History was designed in the Roman style and features a triumphant arch of pink granite and a 350-foot-long paved terrace. Topping the Central Park West façade are four life-size sculptures created by James Earle Fraser of four notable American naturalists and explorers: Daniel Boone, John James Audubon, William Clark, and Meriwether Lewis. Inside the museum, visitors explore exhibits about world cultures, the natural world, and the universe, and behind the scenes, researchers study a world-class collection of more than 34 million specimens and artifacts. In popular culture, this museum is the setting of the 2006 film *Night at the Museum*, with actor Ben Stiller portraying Larry Daley, a security guard who battles exhibits that come to life at night.

STATE OF NEW YORK MEMORIAL TO
THEODORE ROOSEVELT
A GREAT LEADER OF THE YOUTH OF AMERICA
IN ENERGY AND FORTITUDE IN THE FAITH OF OUR FATHERS
IN DEFENCE OF THE RIGHTS OF THE PEOPLE
IN THE LOVE AND CONSERVATION OF NATURE
AND OF THE BEST IN LIFE AND IN MAN
CLARK
LEWIS
TRUTH
KNOWLEDGE
VISION

HARRY F. SINCLAIR HOUSE (UKRAINIAN INSTITUTE OF AMERICA)

LOCATION: 2 East 79th Street

NEIGHBORHOOD: Upper East Side

ARCHITECT: Charles Pierrepont Henry Gilbert

Completed in 1899, this French Gothic–style mansion was built for Isaac Fletcher, a banker and railroad investor. The opulent design was inspired by the William K. Vanderbilt House, a Châteauesque mansion on 5th Avenue. At 20,000 square feet, the house has 27 rooms on six floors. The name is attributed to Harry F. Sinclair, founder of the Sinclair Oil Company, who lived there in the 1920s and 1930s. He was infamously involved in the Teapot Dome scandal. It then became occupied by the Stuyvesant family, descendants of Peter Stuyvesant, who was an early figure in the history of New York City. Since 1955, the Ukrainian Institute of America has owned the building. In popular culture, this house served as the residence of the Valmont family in the film *Cruel Intentions*.

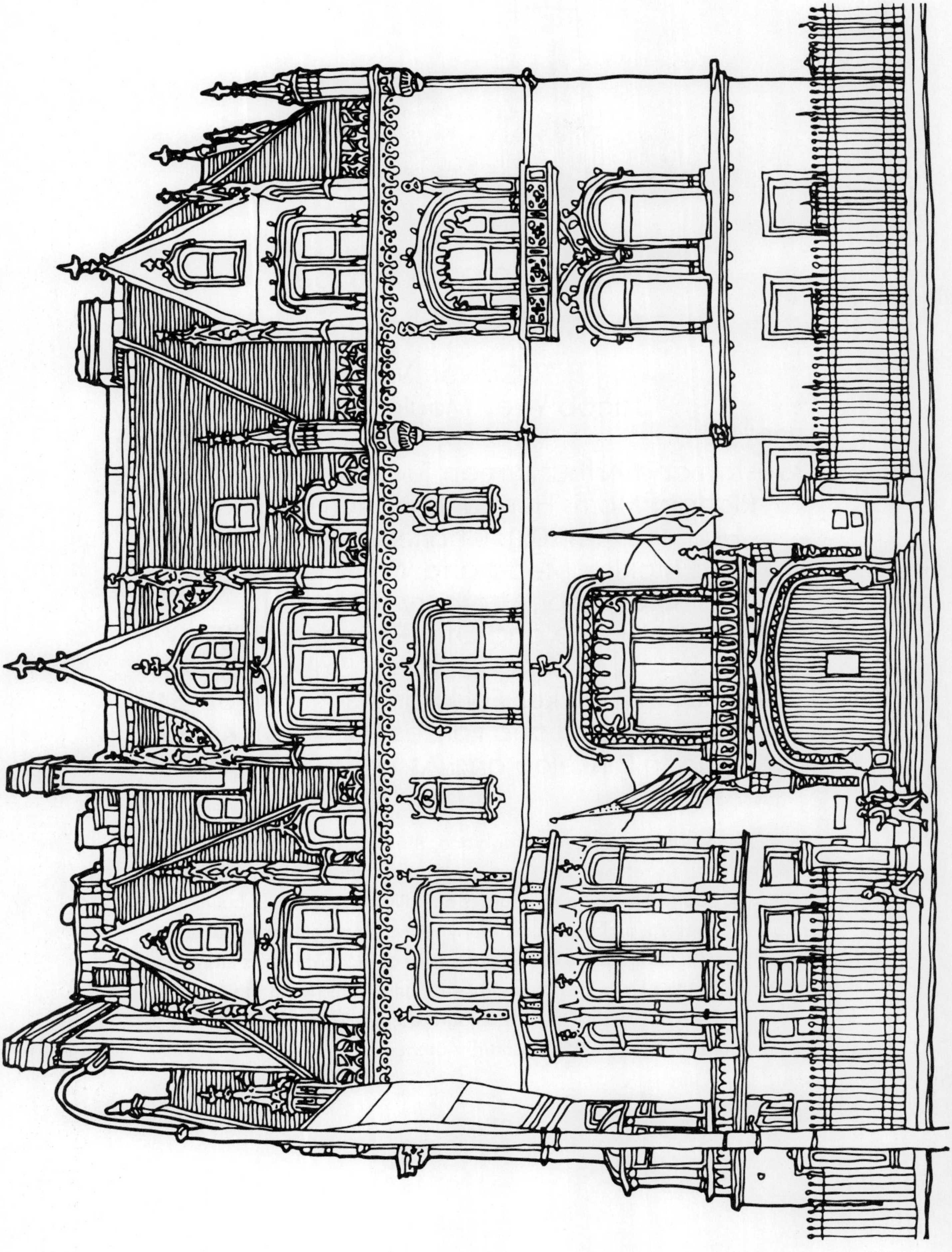

METROPOLITAN MUSEUM OF ART

LOCATION: 1000 5th Avenue

NEIGHBORHOOD: Central Park

ARCHITECTS: Calvert Vaux and Jacob Wrey Mould (1870–1880); Theodore Weston and Arthur Lyman Tuckerman (1880–94); Richard Morris Hunt and Richard Howland Hunt (1894–1902); Charles Follen McKim and McKim, Mead and White (1904–26); Grosvenor Atterbury (1919–24); John Russell Pope and Otto R. Eggers (1929–39); Robert B. O'Connor and Aymar Embury II (1940–54); Vorhees, Walker, Foley and Smith (1952–54); Brown, Lawford and Forbes (1954–65); Kevin Roche John Dinkeloo and Associates (1967–1991)

Located on what was once rural farmland, the Met rests in Central Park on Museum Mile, a stretch of 5th Avenue with prominent cultural institutions and luxury apartments. The museum is actually a collection of buildings designed by several architects over many years. The 5th Avenue façade we see today is attributed to renowned architect Richard Morris Hunt who trained at the École des Beaux-Arts in Paris. Considered the "Dean of American Architecture," Hunt is recognized for his contributions to the architecture profession in 19th-century America.

THE MET
THE MET
NEW YORK
NYPD

SOLOMON R. GUGGENHEIM MUSEUM

LOCATION: 1071 5th Avenue

NEIGHBORHOOD: Upper East Side

ARCHITECTS: Frank Lloyd Wright (1956–59 construction); Gwathmey Siegel and Associates Architects, LLC (1990–92 renovation and addition)

Over 90 feet high, the Oculus skylight at the Solomon R. Guggenheim Museum draws the eye upward as visitors enter a light-filled rotunda. The building is the intersection between two cones. Visitors navigate the rotunda on a spiraling quarter-mile concrete ramp as they view art in this unusual environment. The exterior diameter expands with each rising level and the diameter of the void contracts. Artwork is hung on walls that are set at the same angle as easels and sculptures are placed on a sloping floor, as there are almost no right angles in the building. At the age of 91, Frank Lloyd Wright died before the museum opened to the public in 1959. The museum was designated an official New York City Landmark in 1990, a UNESCO World Heritage Site in 2019, and remains a popular destination for architecture and contemporary art enthusiasts alike.

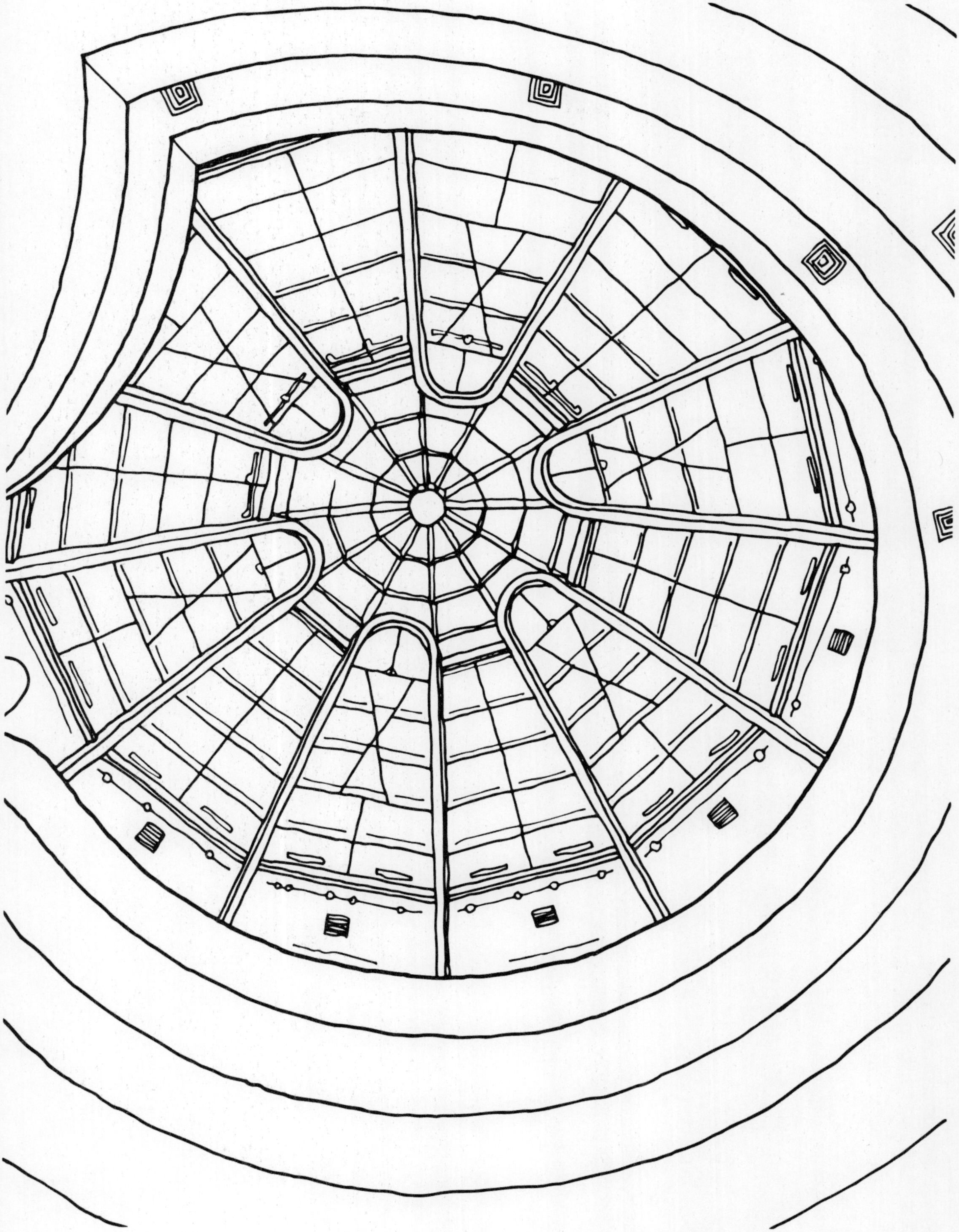